EMBOUCHURE BUILDING

FOR

FRENCH HORN

by

JOSEPH SINGER

as

Compiled and Edited

by

RICHARD E. BALLOU

Preface

This book has been compiled to aid teachers and students in the development of the French Horn embouchure, particularly in the important period following elementary development. It is strongly recommended that the student use this book only under the careful guidance of a capable teacher.

It is based upon the theory, which has been frequently proven by experience, that, mechanically, nearly all of the problems to be met by the player in the orchestra, band, chamber ensemble, etc., can be covered by a comprehensive daily "routine" of practice. (This, of course, does not deal with "musical" problems such as phrasing, expression, etc.).

Various drills (or exercises) which have been numbered in this book have been devised, with no claim to originality, to cope with the various mechanical problems of "embouchure" with which the player is faced in the "field." The teacher should select, from Sections I, II, III, and IV (or V), the exercises most appropriate to the needs of the student.

"Patterns" should be followed so as to cover the full range of the instrument, consistent with the ability of the student. For example, page 19, articulations A, B, C, D, E, and F.

For suggested practice routine, refer to page 40.

The bass clef has been freely used so as to better acquaint the student with it. Examples are given in the "old style" bass clef in which the player plays an octave above the written note. That is,

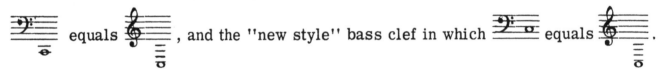

The proper use of the bass clef will be noted before each exercise in which it occurs.

Sections I, II, III, and IV contain "drills," each section of which should be included in a student's normal daily routine. An example of a normal routine could be numbers 1, 7, 24 (with various articulations), and 29 through 35, with other drills in the normal routine to aid specific problems.

It is suggested that number 7 be done daily in all twelve major or minor keys, all on the F horn.* The balance of each day's, or week's, routine should be done in one key, major or minor, for the dual purpose of aiding familiarity with fingering and like problems of that key, and the very important aid to intonation.

Section V contains "drills" that consist of a student's "heavy routine." They should be played in their entirety, with proper rests, for extra stamina. Section V should not be used on a day when orchestral, band or other playing is to be done, but should be a "heavy" workout largely replacing the playing that would come from orchestra and band work.

*Since the F horn has a fuller quality, and is more difficult for response and accuracy, #1 plus this small portion of each day's work should be done exclusively on the F horn. The benefit will prove itself with improved quality and security when the Bb horn is later used. Refer to fingering chart for suggested use of Bb horn.

Fingering Chart

Fingering for F Horn

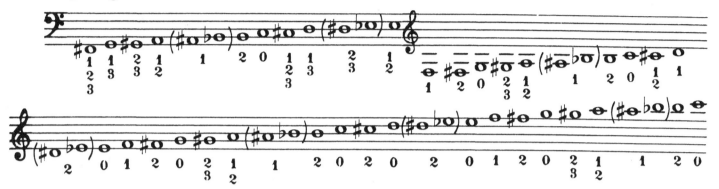

Fingering for B♭ Horn (Sometimes called "B Horn")

Suggested Fingering for F + B♭ Double Horn

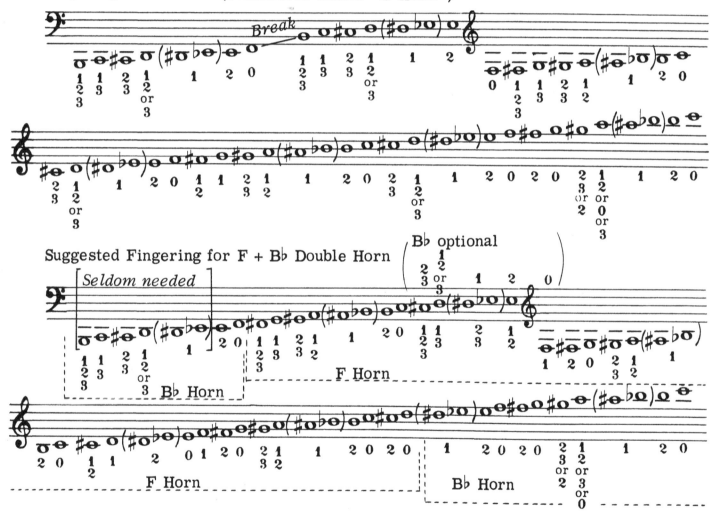

The fingering of the double horn should be done *intelligently*. The *suggested* fingerings can be followed for general use. However, there should not be anything arbitrary about the point of changing to B♭ horn, should the needs of the player call for changing at some other point in the register. *Think.* Use the double horn as a *single* instrument with various fingering possibilities.

EL. 966

Some examples of proper tone (Diagrammed)

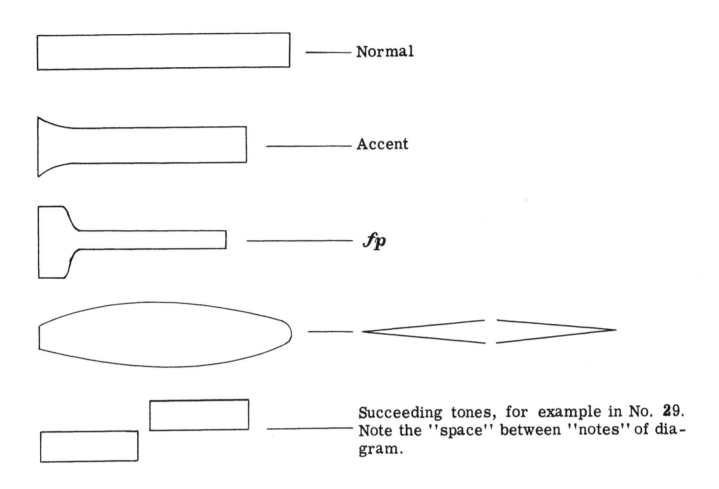

Normal

Accent

fp

Succeeding tones, for example in No. **29**. Note the "space" between "notes" of diagram.

Examples of some of the defects
To Be Avoided

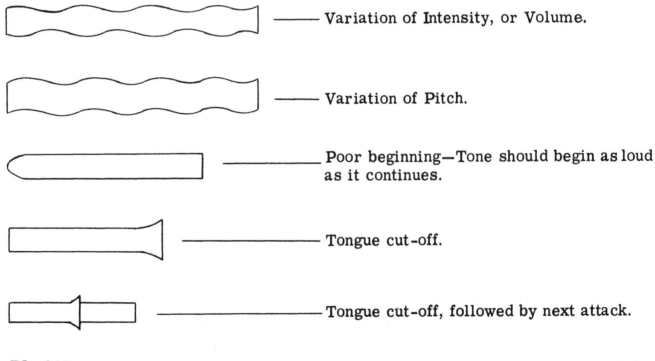

Variation of Intensity, or Volume.

Variation of Pitch.

Poor beginning—Tone should begin as loud as it continues.

Tongue cut-off.

Tongue cut-off, followed by next attack.

SECTION I Tone and Control Studies

(1) can adequately serve as an efficient warm-up, provided the following details are observed:

1. Precise timing of attacks.
2. Clean attacks.
3. Steady full tone at *p-mp* volume.
4. Ending of each note should be controlled — the player should feel able to hold each note much longer than the indicated 2 beats at ♩ = 60.
5. The lips should be completely relaxed after each note is ended so that each succeeding attack serves as a "first note."

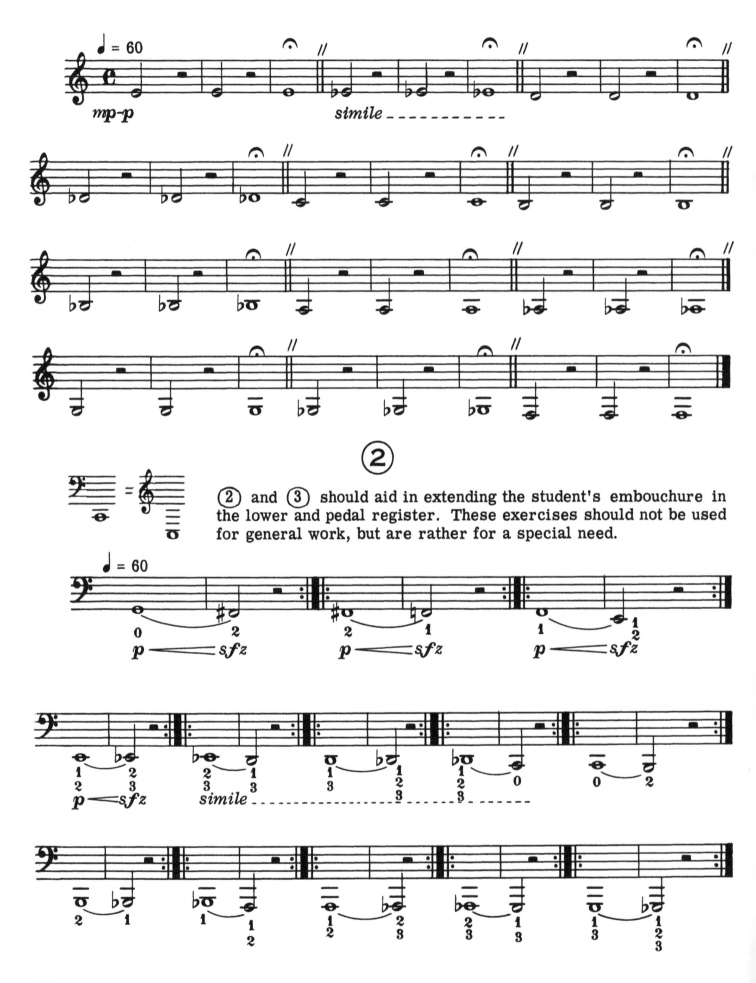

② and ③ should aid in extending the student's embouchure in the lower and pedal register. These exercises should not be used for general work, but are rather for a special need.

③

Optional Low and Pedal Register Exercise.

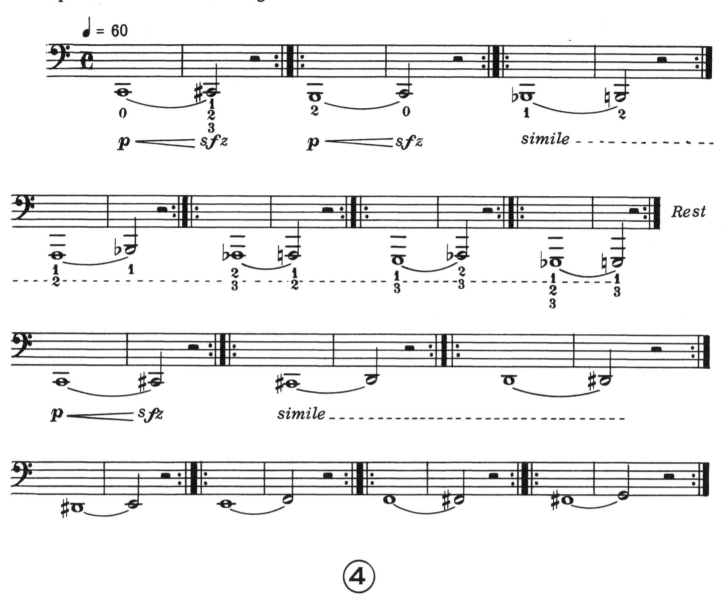

④

④ can be used to aid in avoiding uneven quality. Ideally, the player should strive for the same quality in all registers and at all volumes, except when he specifically wishes a change in quality.

8

⑤ should aid in extending the student's embouchure in the lower and pedal register. This exercise should not be used for general work, but rather for a special need.

Ten Times

Ten Times

Ten Times

Ten Times

Ten Times

EL.966

SECTION II Arpeggio Studies

The arpeggio studies should be done daily in all twelve major (or minor) keys, and exclusively on the F horn. Strive for evenness of attack, dynamics, tempo and quality.

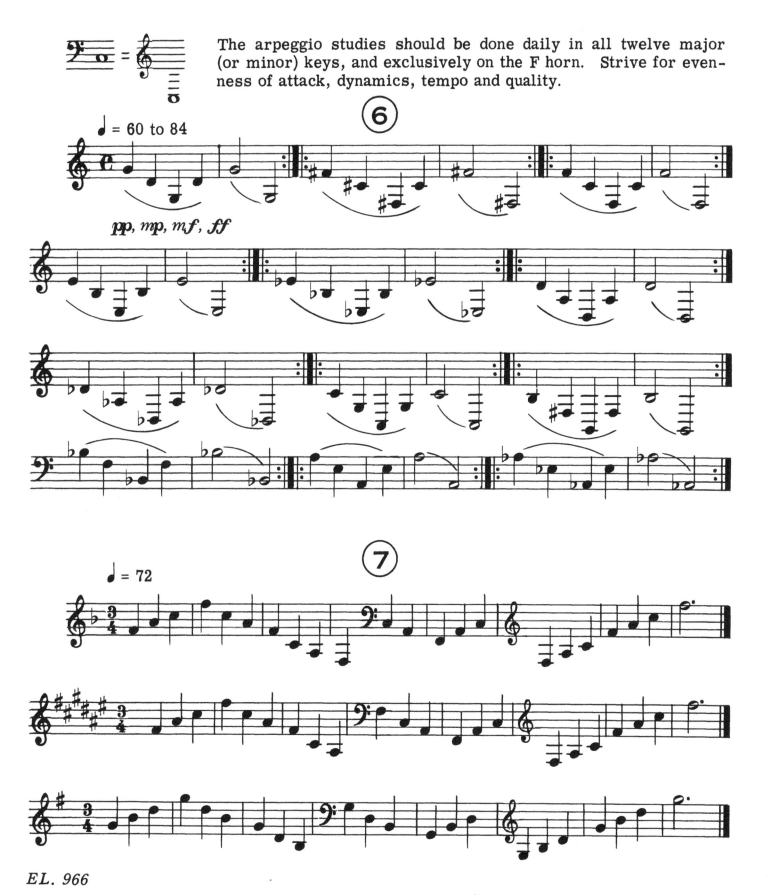

16

EL. 966

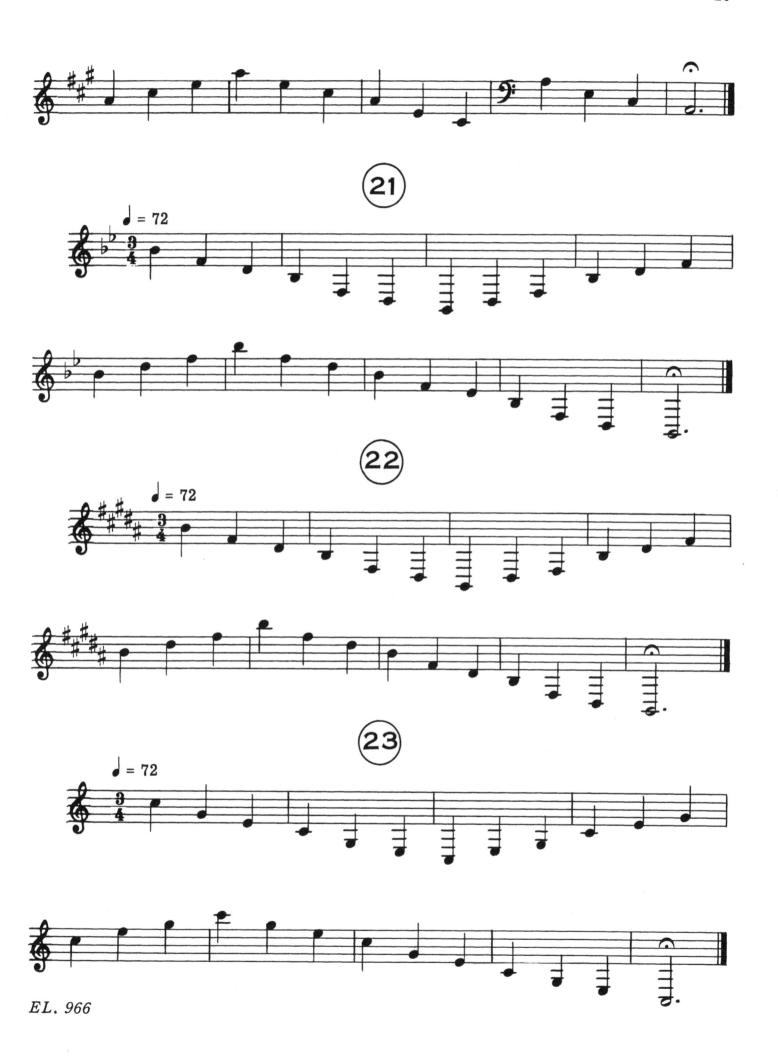

SECTION III   Scale Studies

It is important that the following scale patterns be played in one key per day (or week) with all the various, indicated articulations. The reasons for playing in one key are: (1) to more fully get the feel of the fingerings, and, (2) to aid intonation.

Try to achieve a brilliant staccato at the indicated tempo.   Also, play to the top of the register, even if it is higher than the tonic.

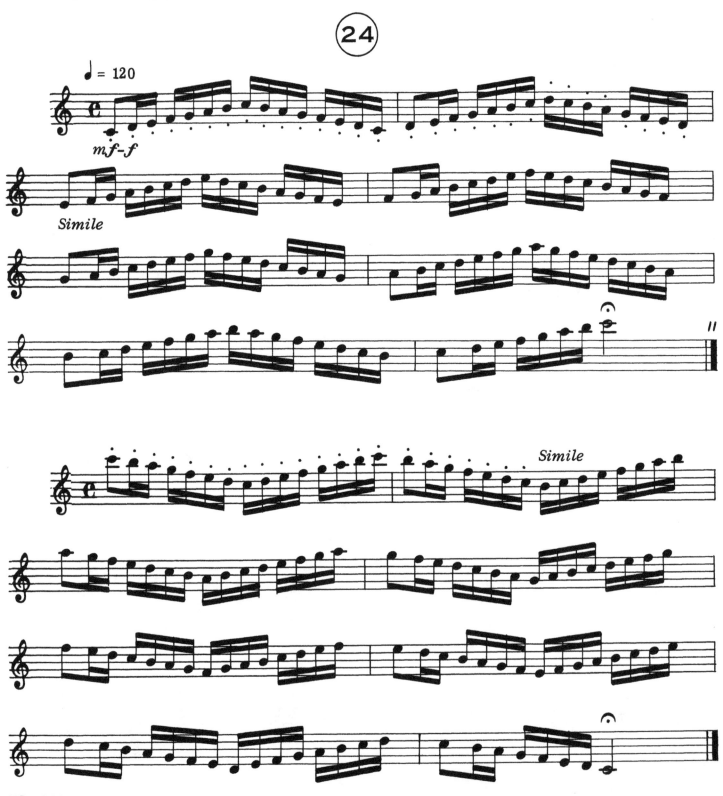

Various Articulations

Simile

㉕

Note extension of scale to top of register

Simile

Simile

Rest

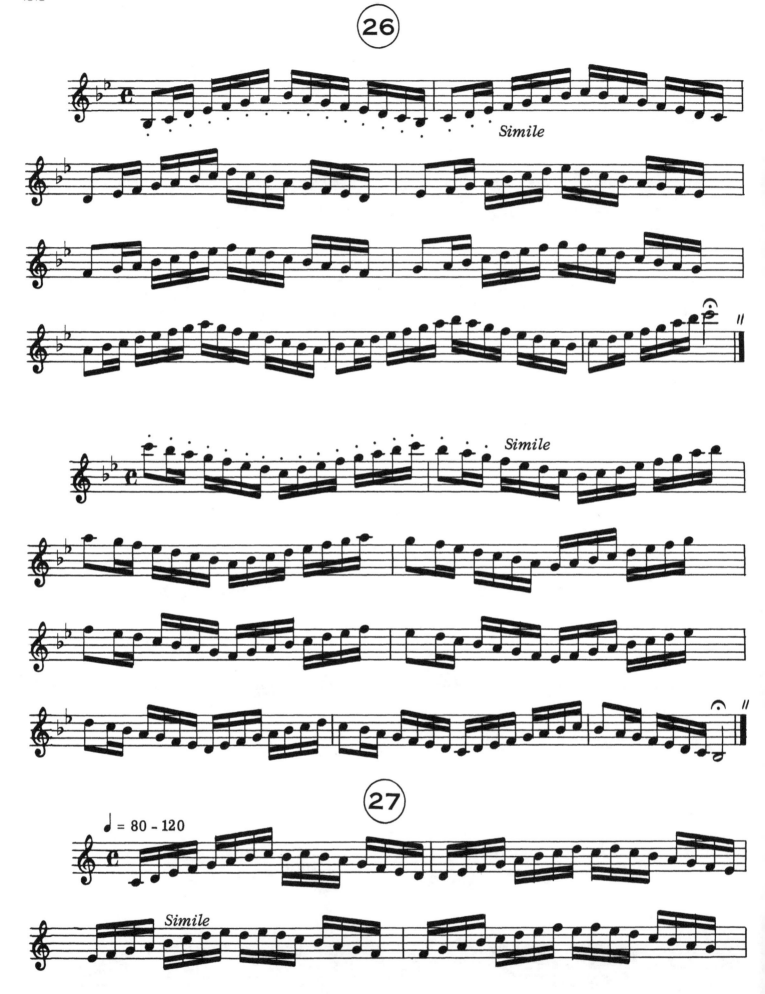

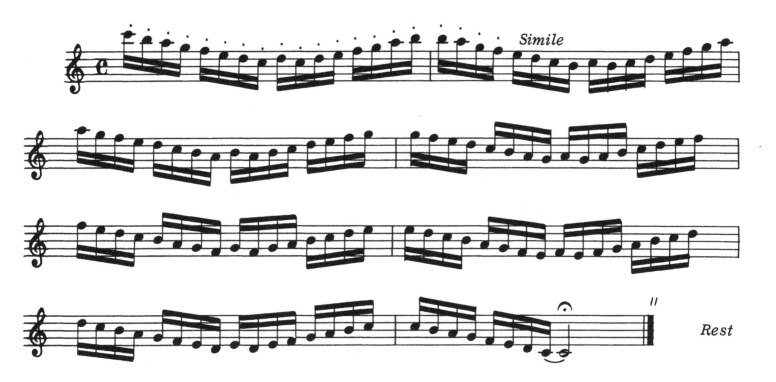

Simile

Rest

Various Articulations

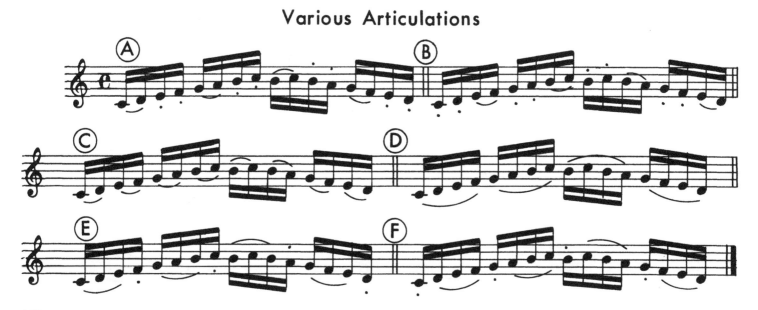

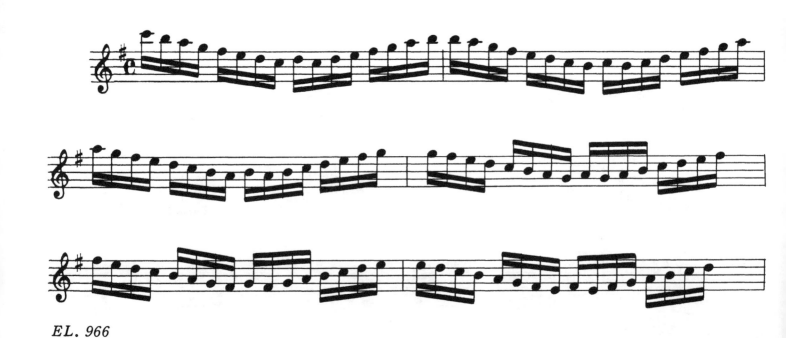

EL. 966

26

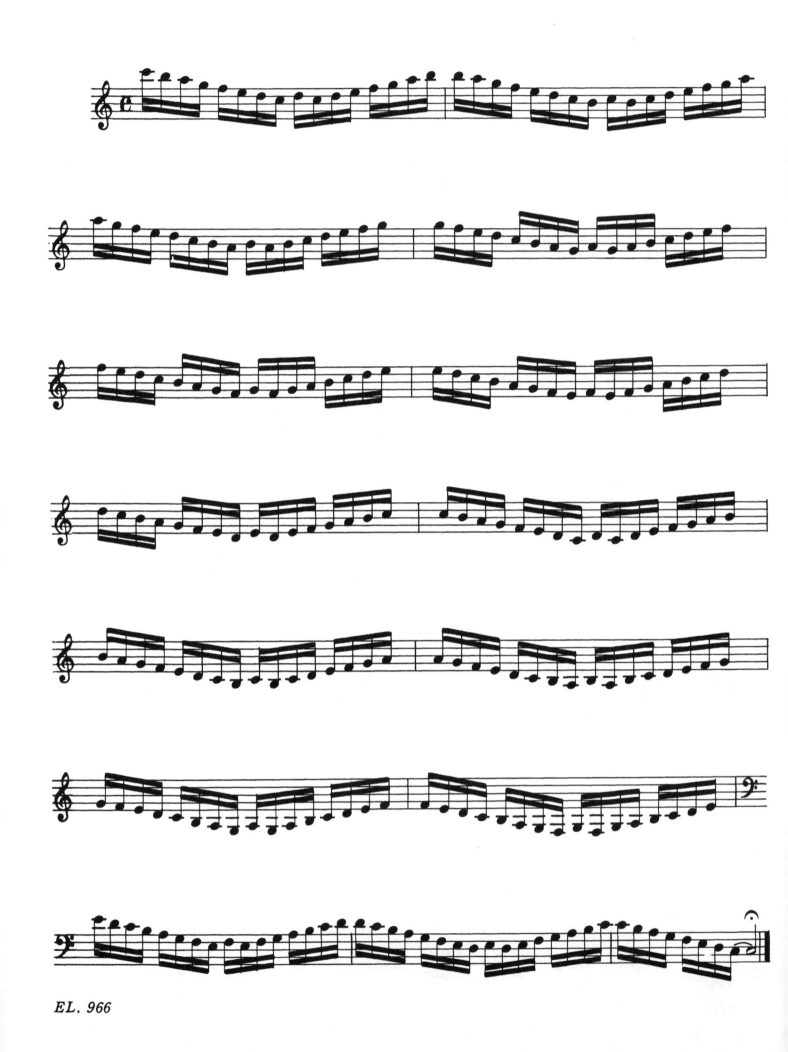

SECTION IV   Intervals

As in practicing scales, the interval studies should be done in one key per day (or week), the same key as the scales. Observe tempo markings as well as the evenness of all notes. (Include all 12 keys, Major and Minor).

28

EL. 966

OCTAVES

(34)

♩ = 84

Also 4 slurred

(35)

TENTHS

♩ = 84

Also 4 slurred

SECTION V   Heavy Routine

This series of exercises has been devised to aid in the building up of (a) still greater stamina and endurance, (b) increased security in the high register, particularly in regard to entrances.

The heavy routine can be used largely to replace the "work-out" that the lips might get from orchestral or band playing.

Except when used partially, this section should be reserved for use on days when the player is doing all of his work at home, and should not be used on days when orchestral or band work is to follow.

Great care should be taken to play (38) with the least possible muscular effort. Concentrate on lip *position* and on being as relaxed as possible. Paradoxical as it may seem, this can be attained after patience and persistance—perhaps after weeks, or even months. It is not easy, but can prove well worth the effort.

(38) should be raised ½ tone after it can be done as written, with relatively easy effort. Several days, or even weeks, later it should again be raised ½ tone in its entirety. However, the student is cautioned not to exceed high C (   ), even though the balance is raised in pitch. Eventually it will become possible to [dependably (!)] enter on high C without any preparation.

Dynamics should be on the "soft" side, but not pinched or squeezed. The tone should be pure, smooth, full and round with the player trying for minimum volume— chiefly because only in this manner can the "feel" of lip position be truly developed, as opposed to dependance on volume and "blowing of air." One should "play"— not "blow."

Ten times for each note

Rest 5 minutes.

(39)

The familiar "long tone" study can give maximum benefit to the embouchure if it is done with measured proportioning of crescendo and diminuendo. Try to build up endurance so that the entire three octaves (or more) can be done without removing mouthpiece from the lips. At first, however, avoid undue strain by resting briefly after two octaves, and by playing the highest notes, if necessary, without crescendo. When playing in various keys, always continue until the highest register of the horn has been reached, rather than ending on the tonic.

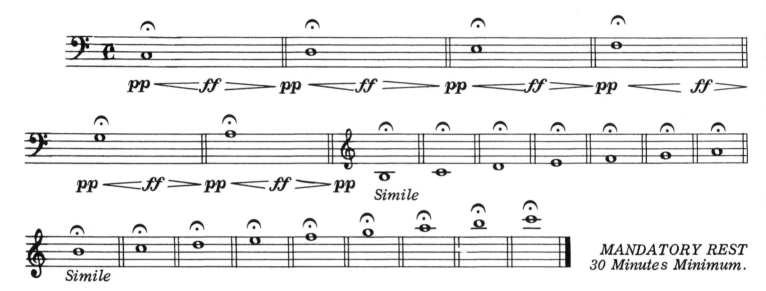

Pattern for playing long tones

For maximum control, the pianissimo should be maintained for one full beat at beginning; fortissimo should be maintained for one full beat. The final pianissimo should be held for at least one full beat. The crescendo and diminuendo should be evenly distributed. [Should be played in key of Day (or Week)].

(40)

To be played first repeating each bar, then without repeats, with each variety of articulation. These scales will be found to be very strenuous, very strengthening and well worth the trouble.

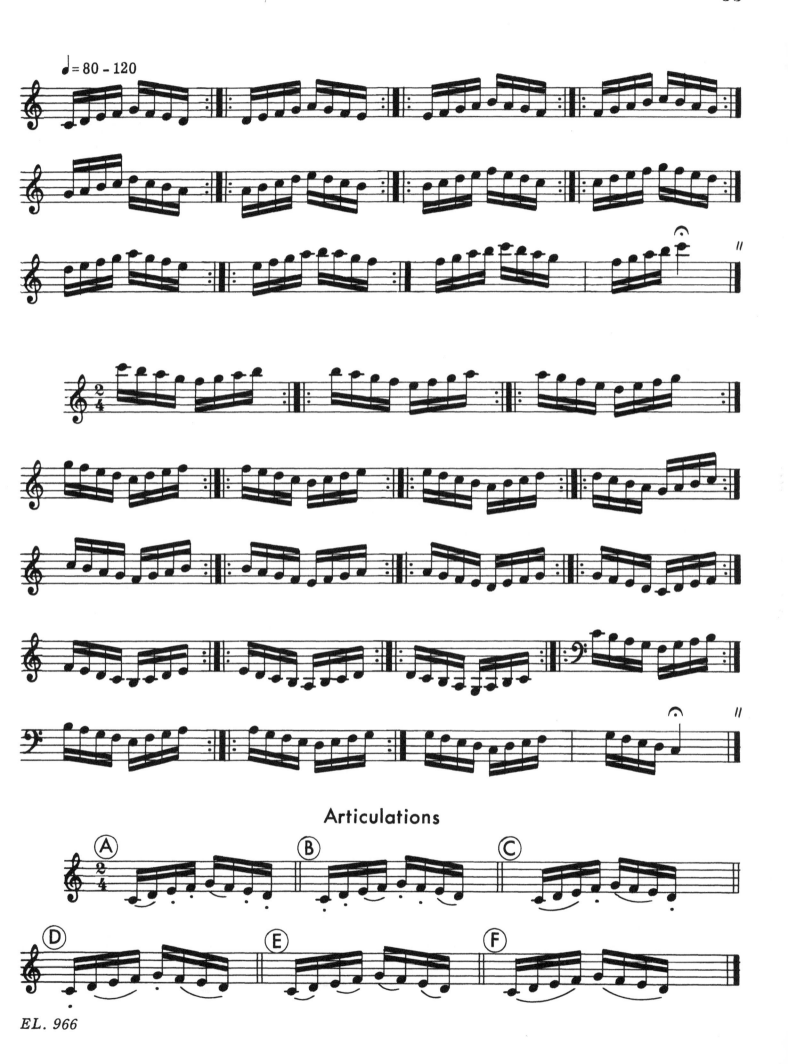

Articulations

Segue

Segue

Segue

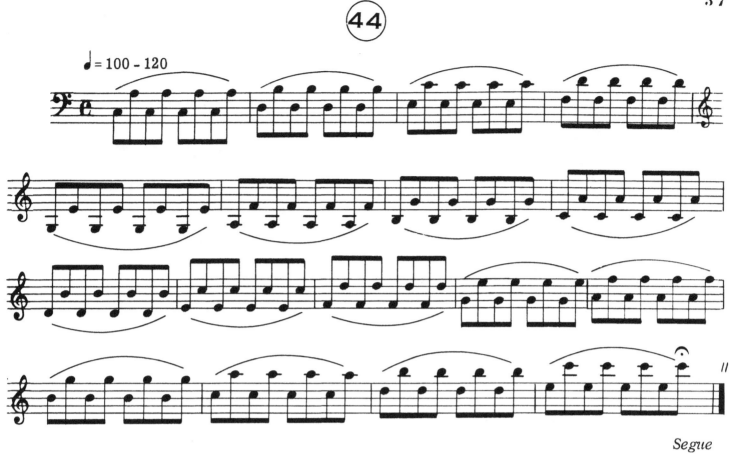

Segue

EL. 966

Segue

(46)

Segue

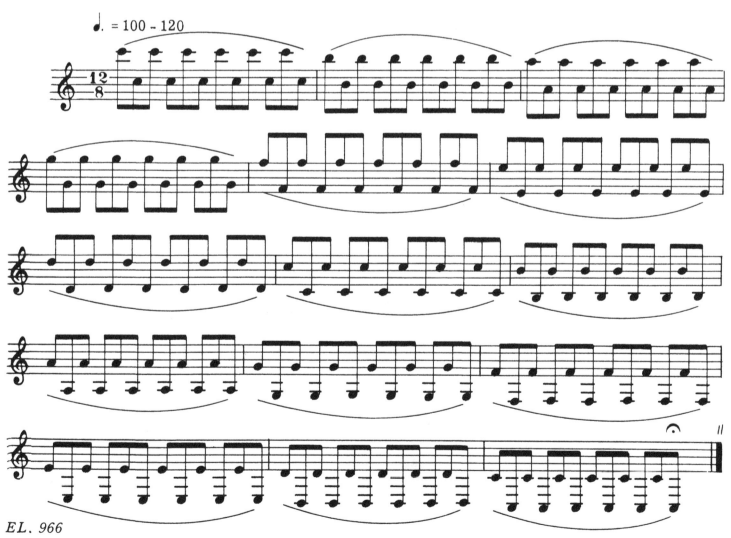

EL. 966

Suggested Practice Routines *

FOR MODERATE ABILITY

<u>EXERCISE NUMBER</u>

1	———	then 5 Minutes Rest.
7	———	then 5 Minutes Rest.
24	———	using all the Various Articulations, then 20 Minutes Rest.

29, 30, 31, 32, 33, 34, 35.

FOR SPECIAL LOW REGISTER NEEDS

1	———	(Using 2nd half of Exercise first) - then 5 Minutes Rest.
2	———	with maximum crescendo—open lips to allow large volume—do not "force" air through lips—try to relax! Then 5 Minutes Rest.
5	———	then 15 Minutes Rest.
or (6, 8, 16, 8.)	———	then 15 Minutes Rest.
24	———	(with optional beginning)—then 30 Minutes Rest.

29, 31, 33, 35.— with appropriate Rests as needed.

FOR INCREASED STAMINA AND POWER
(Should only be used by player with fairly well-developed lips—or under guidance of capable teacher).

38	———	then 10 Minutes Rest.
39	———	then 30 Minutes Rest.
40	———	then 20 Minutes Rest.
41	———	then 1 Minute Rest.
42	———	then 5 Minutes Rest.
43	———	then 1 Minute Rest.
44	———	then 5 Minutes Rest.
45	———	then 1 Minute Rest.
46	———	then 30 Minutes Rest before any further playing!

*The student is advised to play his full "routine" in one key—either major or minor—for a week, or long enough to gain familiarity with the fingering and lip problems of that key—this proceedure also tends to aid intonation. (Sections I & II, of course, are to be practiced as indicated, since chromatic sequence is shown).

N. B. The importance of thorough familiarity with the various keys, both major and minor, cannot be sufficiently emphasized. Practically every passage from "repertoire" can be adequately manipulated with little "unusual" difficulty by the player who has full command of his instrument in all the major and minor keys. It is, therefore, urged that each day's work be comprehensive—cover all the usual needs. Sections III and IV (Scales and Interval-drills, respectively) should be practiced fully each day, with maximum attention to all details of evenness and accuracy. After all major keys have been covered, the student should then study all the minor keys, using both harmonic and melodic minor scales.